My HOLY HOUR

St. Teresa of Calcutta
(Mother Teresa)

A Devotional Journal

Season: _____

Date: _____

Belongs to: _____

My Holy Hour - St. Teresa of Calcutta (Mother Teresa) is part of the *My Holy Hour Devotional Journal Series.* While all journals will have some similar structure and intent, each one will have minor changes to make it unique. Cover image depicts *St. Teresa of Calcutta* when she was at the religious house San Gregorio in Rome (1985).

Go to our website for a free copy of

How to Use a Prayer Journal during Holy Hour
www.HolyHourBooks.com

Holy Hour Books
P.O. Box 430577
Houston, TX 77243

My Holy Hour Devotional Journals

Cover Image by Manfredo Ferrari [CC BY-SA 4.0 (https://creativecommons.org/licenses/by-sa/4.0)], from Wikimedia Commons

ISBN-13: 978-1-941303-83-2
ISBN-10: 1-941303-83-8

First Printing: 2018

Holy Hour Books is an imprint of Ordinary Matters Publishing.

Printed in the United States of America

"Every holy hour we make so pleases the Heart of Jesus that it will be recorded in Heaven and retold for all eternity. It opens up the floodgates of God's merciful Love upon the world."

— Prayer by St. Teresa of Calcutta (Mother Teresa)

Why Keep a Holy Hour

"First, the Holy Hour is not a devotion; it is a sharing in the work of redemption... our Lord asked: 'Could you not watch one hour with Me?'. In other words, he asked for an hour of reparation to combat the hour of evil; an hour of victimal union with the Cross to overcome the anti-love of sin.

Secondly, the only time Our Lord asked the Apostles for anything was the night he went into his agony... As often in the history of the Church since that time, evil was awake, but the disciples were asleep. That is why there came out of His anguished and lonely Heart the sigh: 'Could you not watch one hour with me?' Not for an hour of activity did He plead, but for an hour of companionship.

The third reason I keep up the Holy Hour is to grow more and more into his likeness. As Paul puts it: 'We are transfigured into his likeness, from splendor to splendor.' We become like that which we gaze upon. Looking into a sunset, the face takes on a golden glow. Looking at the Eucharistic Lord for an hour transforms the heart in a mysterious way as the face of Moses was transformed after his companionship with God on the mountain. Something happens to us similar to that which happened to the disciples at Emmaus. On Easter Sunday afternoon when the Lord met them, he asked why they were so gloomy. After spending some time in his presence, and hearing again the secret of spirituality - 'The Son of Man must suffer to enter into his Glory'' - their time with him ended and their "hearts were on fire." — Bishop Fulton Sheen

How to Keep a Holy Hour

"I have found that it takes some time to catch fire in prayer. This has been one of the advantages of the daily Hour. It is not so brief as to prevent the soul from collecting itself and shaking off the multitudinous distractions of the world. Sitting before the Presence is like a body exposing itself before the sun to absorb its rays. Silence in the Hour is a tete-a-tete with the Lord. In those moments, one does not so much pour out written prayers, but listening takes its place. We do not say: 'Listen, Lord, for Thy servant speaks,' but 'Speak, Lord, for Thy servant heareth.'"— Bishop Fulton Sheen

"Know also that you will probably gain more by praying fifteen minutes before the Blessed Sacrament than by all the other spiritual exercises of the day. True, Our Lord hears our prayers anywhere, for He has made the promise, 'Ask, and you shall receive,' but He has revealed to His servants that those who visit Him in the Blessed Sacrament will obtain a more abundant measure of grace." — St. Alphonsus Liguori

Holy Hour Pages

"The purpose of the Holy Hour is to encourage deep personal encounter with Christ."

— *Bishop Fulton Sheen*

5

HOLY HOUR QUOTES

"Nowhere on earth are we more welcomed or loved than by Jesus in Eucharist. When you look at the crucifix, you understand how much Jesus loved you. When you look at the Sacred Host you understand how much Jesus loves you now. This is why we need Perpetual Adoration in every Parish throughout the World."

—St. Teresa of Calcutta

"O God, we believe you are here. We adore you and love you with our whole heart and soul because you are most worthy of all our love.

We desire to love you as the blessed do in heaven ... flood our souls with your spirit and life.

Penetrate and possess our whole being utterly, that our lives may only be a radiance of yours.

Shine through us, and so in us, that every soul we come in contact with may feel your presence in our soul.

Let them look up and see no longer us, but only Jesus!

The fruit of silence is prayer.
The fruit of prayer is love.
The fruit of love is service.
The fruit of service is peace"

— Prayer of Adoration by St. Teresa of Calcutta

Record Your Favorite Quotes Here

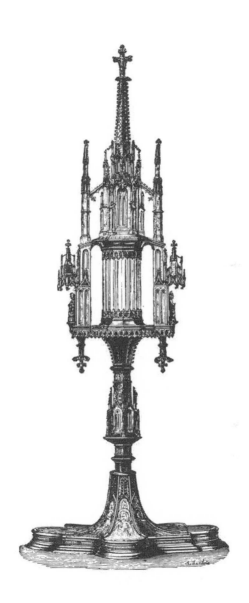

REFLECTIONS

Personal Index

_____ *Pgs* ____

_____ *Pgs* ____

_____ *Pgs* ____

_____ *Pgs* ____

_____ *Pgs* ____

_____ *Pgs* ____

_____ *Pgs* ____

_____ *Pgs* ____

_____ *Pgs* ____

_____ *Pgs* ____

_____ *Pgs* ____

_____ *Pgs* ____

_____ *Pgs* ____

_____ *Pgs* ____

_____ *Pgs* ____

_____ *Pgs* ____

_____ *Pgs* ____

_____ *Pgs* ____

_____ *Pgs* ____

_____ *Pgs* ____

_____ *Pgs* ____

_____ *Pgs* ____

_____ *Pgs* ____

HOLY HOUR JOURNALS

Thank you for your interest in *Holy Hour Journals*. Discover more about using journals to deepen your prayer life by going to our website and getting a free copy of

How to Use a Prayer Journal during Holy Hour
www.HolyHourBooks.com

The Holy Hour Devotional Journal Series has been created to help Catholics from all walks of life to discover, explore, and enjoy the many rewards from a deeper connection to Christ.

Like our Facebook Page:
https://www.facebook.com/HolyHourBooks

Made in the USA
Middletown, DE
03 September 2019